2003 PRESIDENTIAL ADDRESS

IMPRINTED ON THE TICKET

given by

STEVE SKEAVINGTON

To a meeting of the Society at
The European Inn,
Midland Road, Derby
On 21 February 2004
And subsequently repeated at
London Road Station, Brighton
On 19 June 2004

The Transport Ticket Society
2006

Comments etc. regarding this publication are welcome;
please write to the Society
c/o Mr R Davis
42 Hillview Road
Orpington
Kent
BR6 0SF

The production of this publication has been made possible thanks
to the bequest to the Society by the late Robin Pallett
who was a member for about 40 years

ISBN 0 903209 61 6 (978 0 903209 61 8)

Published by
The Transport Ticket Society
c/o Mr R Davis, 42 Hillview Road, Orpington, Kent BR6 0SF

Printed by
Horsham Press

INTRODUCTION

When I was first approached regarding the TTS Presidency for the current year, I had mixed feelings. At first it was fear at the thought of having to prepare a Presidential Address, especially as I'm not due for retirement until 2006 at the earliest and I didn't know how I would have the time for research into a relevant subject. Secondly there was pride at being asked. It is such an honour, so there was no way I was going to refuse - as the opportunity was unlikely to ever be there again.

However the research aspect was not as bad as I had at first feared. Much of it had already been completed in the previous 16 years. Nevertheless, much of this earlier research needed to be revisited and updated. I was amazed at the number of changes to companies over the last decade and a half, with some printers who had traded for very many years ceasing in this period. I can only presume that this is at least partially due to the spread of computer technology, as items that were once printed by commercial printers can now be produced in-house on computers.

Steve Skeavington
July 2006

I must place on record my thanks to the following for their help in my researching printer's imprints

Peter Abel
David Aspinwall
Roger Atkinson
Brian Boddy
Berhard Boreham
Peter Cardno
John Carman
Dilwyn Chambers
E.B.H. Chappell
Geoff Clowes
Barry Cooper
Godfrey Croughton
late John Cunningham
late Trefor David
Bob Davis
David Dodd
Keith Edmondson
late David Edmund
Andrew Fairholm
Michael Farr

Mike Freeman
David Geldard
E.R. Govan
late George Green
Tony Green
David Harman
Brian Hughes
John King
Pat Lidgett
Cyril McIntyre
Roy Marshall
Eric Moles
Tony Newman
Peter Nichols
Christopher Nicholson
Robin Oliver
John Owen
Colin Page
late Robin Pallett
Henry Pryer

David Randell
Martin Rickitt
late Phillip Robinson
Jim Rose
Keith Rowlands
John Scotford
late John Shelbourn
Paul J. Smith
Eric Spencer
Gerritt Van Straaten
Nigel Tarrant
Andrew Waller
Alan Watkins
Glyn Waite
Glyn Weigh
Bob Williamson
Bob Wingrove
Alan Wood

BT Archives, London
St. Brides Printing Library, London

University of Leicester Historic Directories Website
Transport Ticket Society *Journal*

And the following Libraries:-

Brighton & Hove
Derbyshire CC
Devon CC
Exeter Archives
Hampshire CC
Lincolnshire

Manchester
Milton Keynes
Newcastle-upon-Tyne
Nottinghamshire CC
South Yorkshire
West Sussex

*   *denotes illustration included in this publication*

A Challenge.....

In the TTS *Journal* for December 1985, the then Road Editor and Past President Paul Smith, set a competition to find the member with the greatest number of different printers' imprints on tickets in their collections. Paul expressed the wish afterwards that the competition entries might form the basis for a publication regarding printers' imprints. It may well still do so, but at least it now forms the basis of a Presidential Address. Despite an appeal for someone to take this project on board there was no volunteer, so after a bit of gentle arm twisting from Paul I took the project on board and commenced the task of collating the imprints and identifying as many different ones as possible. I was presented with a list of imprints and operators upon whose tickets these imprints appeared but there were no tickets or illustrations of the tickets available. An amazing thing was that all eleven entries to Paul's competition included at least one ticket that no-one else had included. I contacted the ten other entrants to the competition and to my surprise, nine were helpful and supportive. I then started to visit libraries across the length and breadth of the country, searching through old Street and Business Directories. I found the St. Brides printing library useful for printers prior to 1939,as most street directories ceased around this date, and the BT archives useful for printers after about 1940, as prior to this date only larger companies and the very rich had access to telephones.

Some directories I found to be better than others, as I've found printers listed in one directory but not in another, this may be partially due to some directories requiring payment for entries. I also found directories out of date at the time of printing and fossilised errors, which have been repeated in successive directories. A directory bearing the date 1936 was probably printed in 1935 with information up to date to 1934. Places have moved from county to county and you have to know where they were as well as where they are now, for example Newport appears in England under Monmouthshire instead of in the Welsh section. Trade directories also have sections in which printers may be listed other than the obvious printers section, such as account book manufacturers, bookbinders, booksellers, check book manufacturers, newspapers, publishers, stationers, and even railway ticket printers. Sometimes they appear only under one heading, often they appear under more. If anyone has never seen a trade directory I have bought an example with me of Thom's Dublin 1951 directory. The layouts of the directories vary but Kelly's who produced the majority of the directories I have examined are similar. Alexander Thom will be familiar to collectors of CIE tickets as their imprint AT & Co appears on many of their tickets prior to 1962 when they merged to form Hely Thom prior to selling out to Jefferson Smurfit in 1970. There is even a picture of their factory on the back page which is still being used by Smurfit today.

Roger Atkinson also helped by pointing out do's and don'ts regarding research and possible places that might be useful to look to find what I needed to know. This advice was much appreciated and saved hours of otherwise wasted time. I have also helped to boost National Express's profits with journeys to London to carry out research.

All seemed to be going well. I was enjoying the research as this gave me a different aspect of ticket history upon which to concentrate. It would also be one in which at a later date I might hopefully be considered a bit of an authority - as of all other subjects there are many TTS members far more knowledgeable than myself. But then came blow number one: the death of Society librarian George Green. George had promised to help with lending me the imprints that I required from his collection. But now those imprints were lost to me. I re-contacted all the previous entrants that had replied to me and requested photocopies of the imprints in their collections (most but not all obliged.). Some of the photocopies were better and clearer than others. (This is another area of technology that has seen vast improvements over the past 16 years). I also found that the most interesting or rarest imprints always appeared to be on the darkest tickets or poorest quality photocopies. Have I discovered a variation to Murphy's Law?

The death of past TTS President and Chairman John Cunningham was a further blow as it was John who had won Paul's competition by submitting the greatest number of different imprints. Many were so uncommon I could not find examples in other collections. Unfortunately the photocopier John used when he supplied examples to me produced the poorest quality copies that I received. Yet another variation on Murphy's Law! Altogether I have been helped by no fewer than 52 other past or present members of the TTS - which is over 10% of the membership. I hope this will result in as comprehensive list of imprints as is possible.

Whilst researching this subject, new imprints have been discovered on a regular basis. Although the rate has slowed down, probably as most prominent members who are likely to have new imprints have already assisted me, it would be totally unrealistic to believe that other imprints do not exist on travel tickets. In fact I know full well that there *are* other imprints that I have not covered as I have another list of imprints along with operators that issued them. But I have made the rule that if I cannot illustrate the imprint I will not include it. This way I hope to eliminate errors in that I do not wish to introduce errors by reporting imprints that do not actually exist. It is frustrating to do this but I feel that it is the best way to avoid erroneous entries. As I do not personally collect tickets from operators of water-borne services, there is a bias towards tickets from operators of road and of rail services.

Regarding the listing, I have made no attempt to include every different variation of imprint from each printer i.e. Bell Punch Ltd; Bell Punch Co Ltd. etc. Several printers only put their initials on tickets. Fortunately, I have managed to identify virtually all of these printers. I have included company registration numbers for limited companies where these are known although the company name shown is not necessarily the same as when it was first registered. It has been possible for some time to trace a company name forward for a period of up to 20 years but it has only recently been possible to trace a company name back up to 20 years.

Fascinating facts can be discovered during research, such as why did George McCorquodale, a Lancastrian set up a printing works in Wolverton. He started his business in 1841 with a stationers shop in Liverpool and then he opened a printing works in Newton le Willows to service the growing railway industry. In the 1870's he opened a further factory in London. Very logical so far. He was a personal friend of Sir Richard Moon, the then chairman of London and North Western Railway, who persuaded him to open a printing works in the railway town of Wolverton. The reason was to provide employment for the daughters of railwaymen as there was no women's work in Wolverton at this time. McCorquodale's are still in Wolverton today.

What is the legal position regarding printers imprints?

There have been several Acts of Parliament in relation to printers' imprints. The earliest Act that I have traced was passed in 1799 whilst another dates from 1839. The most important was the Newspapers Printers and Reading Rooms Repeal Act of 1869, which restated and continued in force a number of provisions from the earlier Acts. The most recent Act (which only relates to England, Scotland and Wales) was the Printers Imprint Act 1961, which updated aspects of the 1869 Act.

Northern Ireland has the Documents Act (Northern Ireland) of 1970, which whilst not identical is broadly similar, to the above act, although penalties are amongst the aspects that differ from mainland provisions.

The Republic of Ireland, of course, has been subject to its own laws, since its independence from Britain in 1922, although prior to this the earlier Acts would have had application in southern Ireland. Note that I have no knowledge of any legislation passed by the Irish parliament in relation to imprints.

The main purpose behind the introduction of the earlier Acts and especially the 1869 Act, was to prevent the circulation of anonymous and libellous pamphlets without being able to identify their source.

The law regarding printers' imprints as I understand it is as follows (and I've tried to make this as easy to follow as possible and not just quoted the legislation verbatim):

The printers imprint is required on "Any paper or book whatsoever which shall be meant to be published or dispersed". The penalty for omission of the imprint is a fine of up to £25 for each copy and proceedings may be bought in respect of any number of copies. Those liable are the printer and any person who publishes and disperses, or assists in publishing or dispersing the offending material. Prosecutions must be begun within three months of the date of printing (in the case of a printer) or date of publication or sale, (in the case of a publisher or distributor). If the imprint is required by law on a particular piece of printed matter, the printer must add it whether the customer agrees or not. A test case held in 1822 decided that," The omission of the imprint even by desire of the customer, disentitled the printer to recover payment for the work done, in addition to rendering him liable to penalty."

Under printers' imprint legislation, a printer in Great Britain must keep for a period of six months a copy of everything he prints for reward. If it is of the kind required to bear a printers imprint, he must also write or print on that copy the name and address of the person or persons who employed him to print it, and must at any time produce on demand within that time period a copy on demand to any magistrate. Magistrates who are members of the TTS please note!

I have obtained tickets for my own collection courtesy of two printers whom I contacted during my research that they no longer required as the time limits had expired for their retention.

As with all laws there are exemptions and this legislation seems to have more than most. Amongst the exemptions from printers imprints are:

- Matter which is not meant to be published or dispersed: ie. such as things printed for in-house internal circulation only.

- Matter which comprises words calculated to convey only a greeting, invitation, or other message in conventional form. This would appear to me to include amongst other things: Christmas cards, greeting cards, birthday cards, stationery sheets, letterheads, postcards, record books, cartons, carrier bags, address books, compliment slips, invitation cards, envelopes, card index systems, not forgetting things like stamp albums, photograph albums, and especially albums for ticket collections.

- Matter which comprises a drawing, illustration or other picture provided the picture represents only a geometrical, floral, or other design or a registered trademark or a combination thereof i.e. certain Christmas cards, greeting cards and such items as serviettes.

- Matter consisting of the name and address or business or profession of any person and the articles in which he deals or the services he offers, and any papers for the sale of estates, or goods by auction or otherwise, i.e. business cards, address cards, mail order catalogues, auction catalogues, estate agents brochures.

- Papers printed by the authority, and for the use of either house of parliament

- And to us the most important group of exemptions –other matter specifically exempted:

o   Bank of England notes (no mention though of Bank of Scotland, Royal Bank of Scotland or Clydesdale bank notes).
o   Stamps
o   Bills of exchange and promissory notes
o   Bonds and other securities for payment of money
o   Bills of lading
o   Insurance policies
o   Letters of attorney, deeds and agreements
o   Transfers
o   Assignments or dividend warrants of corporation or company stocks or securities
o   Court proceedings
o   Papers printed by authority of public boards or public officers in the execution of their duties.
o   Receipts for money or goods.

As a transport ticket is a receipt for money or goods, it has therefore been exempted by parliament from having a printers imprint. Fortunately many tickets despite legally not requiring an imprint have one - otherwise this would be a very short Presidential Address, and it would have made research by members of the society into identifying printers much harder if not impossible. It can be hard enough now as articles over the years by Roger Atkinson in particular have demonstrated, and many of those tickets had an imprint but not of the actual printer. The names of Harry Gilbert ,Whiting, and Harland immediately spring to mind. I have to caution care as the imprint on the ticket is not necessarily that of the printer of the ticket, as often this work is subcontracted out to specialist printers and the imprint is often that of the printer with whom the original order was placed.

Williamsons of Ashton along with the previously mentioned printers seem to be the main culprits of this practice. Indeed tickets printed by Alfred Williamson are known with the customer reference number A91 on tickets of Hythe Pier Electric Railway; This is actually the customer reference number of Archer Press. Indeed after Archer Press changed its name to Reynolds printers, tickets of Hythe Pier Electric Railway continued to show A91 but now along with the imprint of Reynolds. Note that my research is only in printer's imprints and not into who actually printed the ticket.

So far I am able to provide illustrations of 518 different imprints and in addition to this I am aware of several others that exist which I cannot yet illustrate. Tickets bearing over half of the imprints of which I am aware are represented by examples in my own collection.

I was asked to try to limit this Address to between 1½ and 2 hours, i.e. 120 minutes at most.

I am now some way into my presentation and to scale the remainder of the Address down to about 10 seconds per ticket would clearly not work, so how was I to present the remainder of this Address?

I thought of a previous Presidential Address by Eric Moles, who concentrated on English post bus tickets for his talk and then produced Scotland and Wales later. I propose to do the opposite to Eric and cover Scotland and Wales today as the total number of imprints amounts to 75 which is manageable, whereas the 400 English imprints is not, and will have to wait for another occasion, probably after my retirement. I also have 33 Irish imprints and a further 10 from the Isle of Man and the Channel Islands to incorporate somehow.

Unfortunately Scotland accounts for some of the poorest photocopies of imprints partly because John Cunningham had a bias towards Scottish independents that no-one else seems to have in their collections. Hopefully this presentation will result in better quality specimens becoming available in due course.

As you are no doubt aware, our American cousins, for some long forgotten reason long, long ago decided that the format of dates used by everybody else on the planet of day/month/year needed revising to month/day/year. This was not a problem until Mrs. Gates gave birth to young Billy, who in later years got involved with computers. So rich and powerful did Billy get as his computers eventually controlled the entire planet. Fiendishly and illogically (he was not a Star Trek fan) Billy decided to stick to the utterly illogical American date format despite the fact that the rest of the world use the logical one. However as I am British I'm sticking with the day/month/year convention.

SCOTTISH IMPRINTS

1.* The imprint **Allan and Ferguson** is known on a ticket of Glasgow and Ayr Railway. This is the imprint of David Allan and William Ferguson. David Allen traded alone from 1832-1834 at 187, Trongate Glasgow. In 1835 he was joined by William Ferguson and they traded as Allan & Ferguson from this address. From 1836-1843 they traded from 57, Argyle Street, Glasgow and from 1844-1847 at Turners Court, 87, Argyle Street, Glasgow. In 1848 they moved to 74, Buchanan Street, Glasgow, and from 1849-1851 to 70, Buchanan Street and 1852-1874 to 74, Buchanan Street Glasgow. In 1875 until at least 1924 they were based at 126, Renfield Street, Glasgow. They had vanished from directories by 1936. In 1838 there was also an address at 97, High Street, Paisley.

2.* The imprint printed and donated by **C. Billette**, Glasgow is known on the reverse of a special tour ticket valid on 28/4/1984, issued on Blackpool tramways. Charles Billette of Hillhead, Glasgow is also known to have printed tickets for Western Scottish, and Heaton Park Tramway in Manchester, these bore the imprint Viking. This information was supplied to me by John Owen, as I was unable to find any trace of these printers in the more usual directories. Billette of course is French for ticket. The only ticket I have with the Viking imprint is a printer's specimen.

3.* The imprint **B&H Ltd** is known on an exchange ticket of Western SMT Co Ltd of Kilmarnock issued in 1953.This is believed to be the imprint of Bone & Hulley. Bone & Hulley had ceased trading by 1970 so I have been unable to confirm this with them, I contacted Western Print, the in-house printing department of Western Scottish, who were reasonably certain that this was the printer, but could not give me 100% confirmation. Bone & Hulley were at 35, Dundas Street, Glasgow by 1916 and were still there as late as 1960.

4.* The imprint **JB&G Glasgow** is known on a punch ticket of Western SMT of Kilmarnock. This is the imprint of John Brown and Gray who were trading at 44, Clyde Place, Glasgow, by 1931 and were still there in 1939. John Brown and Gray had vanished from directo ries by the 1950's.

5.* The imprint **Caithness Printers, Wick** is known on a ticket of Morrison's Coaches issued during 1988. Caithness Printers had premises situated at Unit 4B, Airport Industrial Estate, Wick, Caithness. Caithness Printers Ltd (SC122512) was dissolved on 14/7/1992.

6.* The imprint **R.Dinwiddlie, Dumfries** is known on a ticket of R.Murray and Son of Stranraer, Robert Dinwiddie had premises situated at 117/119, High Street, Dumfries, and was at these premises by 1924 and still there in 1975, although he is no longer trading.

7. The imprint **Elmbank Printing Services, Peebles** is known on the reverse of a student's pass of Nationwide Coaches of Lanark. Elmbank Printing Services had premises situated at 65, Edderston Road, Peebles at the time the ticket was printed, but have since moved to premises situated at 8, Elcho Street Brae, Peebles EH45 8HU.

8. The imprint **Gellatly, Edinburgh** is known on a ticket of North British Railway. John Gellatly was born in Forfar on 20/10/1802 and died in Edinburgh on 26/4/1859. He traded in 1827 from 186, Rose Street, Edinburgh then in 1828 and 1829 from 8, West Register Street Edinburgh, from 1830-1836 he was at 10, West Register Street Edinburgh. From 1837-1842 at 44, West Register Street Edinburgh and from 1843-1845 at 1 George Street, Edinburgh. From 1846-1860 the address was 26, George Street, Edinburgh. After John Gellatly's death the business was carried on under the same name by Robert Whyte. However from 1861-1871 the name was changed to Gellatly and Whyte still trading from 26, George Street, Edinburgh. I can find no trace of this firm after 1871.

9.* The imprint **T.M.Gemmell & Son Ltd**. is known on an employee's privilege ticket of AA Motor Services Ltd of Ayr. T.M.Gemmell & Son Ltd were registered on 9/6/1938 (SC20456) and ceased printing during 1982. The company was dissolved on 16/3/1993. Gemmell had premises situated at 100, High Street Ayr where he was based in 1975 and later at Whitfield Drive, Heathfield, Ayr KA8 9RX, which was his last premises. Searches of directories prior to 1970 can find no trace of this printer which as the company was registered in 1938 may signify a change of name or location.

10. The imprint **Gilchrist & Munro, Glasgow** is known on a punch ticket of Alexander's Motor Service. Gilchrist & Munro are no longer trading. Despite trawling through Glasgow trade directories and printers directories I have been unable to find any trace of this printer. I did find trace of William Gilchrist at 64, West Howard Street, Glasgow and William Munro at both 81, Virginia Street and 80, Gordon Street, Glasgow in Glasgow who were both trading as printers in the 1930's but I do not know if they have any connection with Gilchrist & Munro.

11.* The imprint **G. Girdwood** is known on a ticket of Dundee, Perth & Aberdeen Railway Junction Co. George Girdwood was born in 1796 and died in 1861. Girdwood commenced trading in 1850. George Girdwood & Co (Dundee) Ltd (company SC24868) was registered on 23/12/1946 and is still trading from 2, Lower Pleasance, Dundee, DD1 5QU from where they've been since at least 1983. Earlier addresses include 17, Reform Street, Dundee (1872-1876); 7, Albert Square, Dundee (1880); 70-74, Commercial Street, Dundee (1885); 53, Meadowside, Dundee (1889-1916); 3, Panniure Street, Dundee, (1919-1931); 62, Murraygate, Dundee (1936-1955); 47, Perth Road. Dundee (1960-1971) and 160, Perth Road, Dundee (1973-1980).

Glasgow and Ayr Railway.

IRVINE TO **AYR.**

Second Class.

462

The Company will NOT BE RESPONSIBLE for passengers' LUGGAGE unless regularly BOOKED IN THE OFFICE.

(1) Allan and Ferguson

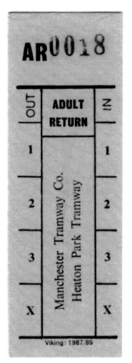

AR 0018

OUT	ADULT RETURN	IN
1		1
2	Manchester Tramway Co. Heaton Park Tramway	2
3		3
X		X

Viking: 1987.85

(2) (35)

Y 6394

Western S.M.T. Co. Ltd.

MOTOR OMNIBUS.

EXCHANGE TICKET

Not to be accepted for cash.

This ticket has no value unless accompanied by the top portion of a Return Ticket of the same value.

J. B. & G. Glasgow.

(4) J.B. & G.

P MORRISON'S COACHES

Issued subject to operator's rules & regulations

PASSENGER'S COPY   Caithness Printers, Wick, Tel: 3386

O.A.P./RETURN

1p	2p	3p	4p	5p	6p	7p	8p	9p	10p	20p	30p	40p	50p

£10 | £9 | £8 | £7 | £6 | £5 | £4 | £3 | £2 | £1 | 90p | 80p | 70p | 60p

8677

RETURN/O.A.P.

To be handed into office by conductor

CONDUCTOR'S COPY   Caithness Printers, Wick, Tel: 3386

C

1p	2p	3p	4p	5p	6p	7p	8p	9p	10p	20p	30p	40p	50p

O.A.P. £10 | £9 | £8 | £7 | £6 | £5 | £4 | £3 | £2 | £1 | 90p | 80p | 70p | 60p

8677

(5) Caithness Printers

The Dundee & Perth & Aberdeen Railway Junction Co.

FREE PASS .... **CLASS. NOT TRANSFERABLE.**

No. **51**

18

The Guards will permit

to pass *from* .... *to* ....

G. Girdwood, Printer, Dundee.

NOTE.—Any Party, other than the Person named herein, using this Pass, is liable to the penalties which a Passenger incurs by travelling without having paid his Fare.

This Pass is issued on the condition that no claim whatever be made on the Company, in the event of accident or injury to the holder, or damage to his or her property, whilst travelling on the Dundee and Perth, or Dundee and Newtyle Railways.

(11) G Girdwood

12. **Glasgow Numerical Printing** was founded by Alec Carlaw in 1878 with the aid of his father David Carlaw. David Carlow had premises at 75, East Howard Street, Glasgow in 1872, but by 1889 had moved to 81, Dunlop Street, Glasgow (office) and 54-58, Ropewalk Lane, Glasgow (factory). Glasgow Numerical Printing Co is first seen in Kelly's 1889 directory also at 54-58, Ropewalk Lane, Glasgow but by 1900 they had moved to 31, Finnieston Street, Glasgow. They also had premises at 30, Williamson Street, Liverpool in 1904 and 2, Fen Court, London in 1914, where they were listed as Glasgow Numerical Ticket and Checkbook Printing Co. The company was purchased circa 1980 by Henry Booth (Hull) Ltd and the company name was changed to GNP-Booth Ltd. Production continued at both Glasgow and Hull and a move to a modern factory at New Albion Estate, Halley Drive, Yoker, Glasgow G13 4DL followed Booth's move to a new factory in Hull. Research in company names gets complicated and the situation I found is as follows; Company SC26956 was registered on 30/3/1949, I do not know what this company was originally called however it had become GNP-Booth Ltd and on 19/3/1991 changed its name to Glasgow Numerical Printers Ltd and again on 16/1/1995 to The 48 Hour Pin Company Ltd and yet again on 7/4/1999 to Bourne Promotions Ltd based in Dalkeith. This company is currently dormant. Another company SC128244 was registered on 6/11/1990 and was then known as Boydslaw (35) Ltd which on 19/3/1991 became GNP Booth Ltd (no hyphen) and on 8/5/1997 became GNP Booth (no 2) Ltd the registered office of this company is situated at the New Albion Estate address. Company SC172936 was registered on 26/2/1997 as Dalglen (no659) Ltd and on 8/5/1997 became GNP Booth Limited (again with no hyphen). This company is currently in liquidation with the registered office listed as c/o Kroll Ltd, of Glasgow who are accountants. An earlier limited company The Glasgow Numerical Printing Company Limited was trading by 1899. David Carlow & Sons Limited was listed in 1939 at 31, Finnieston Street, Glasgow under the heading, Numerical printing machine makers.

13. **Arthur Guthrie & Sons Ltd Printers, Ardrossan** is known on a ticket of Clyde Coast Services Ltd of Saltcoats, Ayrshire. Arthur Guthrie and Sons were based at 64 Princes Street Ardrossan Ayrshire from 1872 until at least 1962. They also had premises at Herald Street, Ardrossan, which was first seen listed in directories in 1955 and they remained there until the company ceased trading sometime after 1984. Arthur Guthrie and Sons Ltd, Company SC11342 was dissolved on 10/5/1988.

14.* The imprint **Thomas Houston & Co Ltd** is known on the reverse of a ticket of Hutchison's Coaches, (Overtown) Ltd. Thomas Houston & Co Ltd (SC55182) was registered on 5/3/1974. The only known premises were situated at 34, North Vennel, Lanark, Strathclyde, ML11 7LY, from where they were trading by 1970. The company changed its name on 23/6/1997 to T H Management Ltd. And was dissolved on 8/12/1999.

15.* The imprint **J.O.E. Lockerbie** is known on a weekly ticket of Blue Band motor Service. J.O.E. was the imprint of Jarvis Office Equipment of 3/5, Station Road Lockerbie, Dumfriesshire. Directories list GB Jarvis Ltd at 7, Station Road, Lockerbie in 1970. By 1975 Brian Jarvis printer is listed at this address, and by the mid 1980's he was trading as Jarvis Office Equipment. The company has ceased trading in the last decade.

16.* The imprint **Largs Printing Co** is known on the reverse of a ticket of Clyde Coast Services Ltd of Saltcoats Ayrshire obtained by me on a visit to their depot in 1981. Largs Printing Co were founded in 1969 and have premises situated at 120, Main Street Largs Ayrshire KA30 8JN.

17.* The imprint **Wm. MacDonald, Edinburgh** is known on a parcel ticket of Scottish Omnibuses Ltd of Edinburgh. Wm MacDonald and Co Ltd was first seen listed in Kelly's 1900 directory with premises situated at 8, St. Giles Court, Edinburgh, but by 1904 they had moved to London Road, Edinburgh and they were still there in 1944, however by 1947 they had moved to 7, Abbey Street, Edinburgh 7. They were still at these premises in 1971, but had ceased trading by 1977. There were also premises at 120/126, Portland Street, Manchester. MacDonald's also printed many of the directories that I consulted whilst researching printers imprints.

18.* **Alex MacKay (Printers and Stationers) Ltd**, (company SC44328) was registered on 20/2/1967. Tickets of Peter Harte Coaches have been seen showing the addresses 35, Princes Street, Port Glasgow and 5-7, Fore Street, Port Glasgow, although the same telephone number is used on both tickets. The company is currently in liquidation the last accounts being filed during 1996.

19.* The imprint **John McKinlay, Printer, Perth** is known on a season ticket of Earnside Coaches, Glenfarg, Perth. John McKinlay Ltd (company SC80840) was registered on 15/11/1982 with premises situated at 11/15 King Street, Perth, PH2 8HR. On 1/8/2000 there was a minor change of company name to John McKinlay (Printers) Ltd.

20.* The imprint **MacLure and MacDonald** is known on a ticket of Glasgow, Paisley & Greenock Railway. Andrew MacLure (1812-1885) and Archibald Gray MacDonald traded from 1836-1838 at 190, Trongate, Glasgow. From 1838-1852 they traded from 57, Buchanan Street, Glasgow moving to 20, Vincent Street Glasgow from 1853-1884, and again in 1885 to 2, Bothwell Circus Glasgow, by 1904 they had moved to 164, Bothwell Street, Glasgow where they remained until at least 1931. By 1936 they were at 2-10 Carrick Street, Glasgow and they remained there until they ceased trading. In 1840 they were joined by A McGregor and for a time traded as MacLure, MacDonald & McGregor, but by 1874 were back trading as MacLure & MacDonald. There were also premises at 37, Walbrook, London in 1862/3.

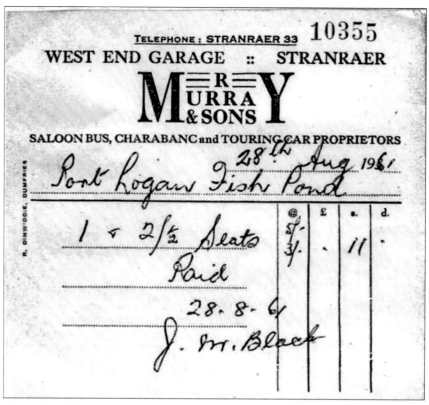

(6) R. Dinwiddie

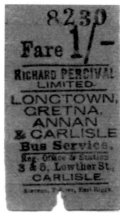

(33) Stevens, East Riggs

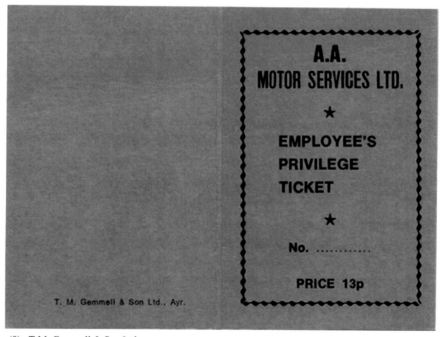

(9) T.M. Gemmell & Son Ltd

(15) J.O.E.

HUTCHISON'S COACHES (Overtown) LTD.   (10)
This Ticket is accepted by the Holder on the following conditions:—
    1   It is subject to General Regulations as printed in published Time-Table.
    2   It is available for one Return Journey per day for five consecutive days
excluding Saturday and Sunday unless otherwise authorised.
    3   The Company does not undertake that any bus shall start or arrive at the
time specified in their time-tables and reserves the right to alter the Time-Tables
at any time, and they shall not be responsible for any loss, damage, or inconvenience
arising from such failure to start, delay in arrival, or Time-Table
alteration, or from lack of accommodation on any vehicle.
                    THOMAS HOUSTON & CO. LTD

(14) Thomas Houston & Co. Ltd.

Clyde Coast Services Ltd.

TO BE SHOWN ON DEMAND
NOT TRANSFERABLE

Largs Printing Co.,120 Main St., Largs

(16) Largs Printing Co.

Premises were also known at 77A, Market Street, Manchester (1852-1876), 57, Princes Street, Manchester (1877), and 16, Fenwick Street, Liverpool (1863-1876) which were managed by A McGregor. MacLure & MacDonald Limited (company SC5910) was dissolved on 23/12/1997.

21. The imprint **David McMillan Printer, Dumfries** is known on a season ticket of Carruthers Bus Service, New Abbey. David McMillan had premises at 6, Friars Vennel, Dumfries DG1 2RN, by 1893 and he is still trading from these premises today. He also had additional premises at 32, Whitesands, Dumfries which was seen listed in 1893 and at 51,English Street, Dumfries by the late 1980's. Directories from the 1970's onwards list them as sellers of fishing tackle as well as printers. McMillan's who are still trading are now just fishing tackle sellers and no longer printers.

22. The imprint **J. McQueen & Son, Galashiels** is known on a punch ticket of Brook & Amos Ltd. Galashiels. John McQueen's was at 25/27, Channel Street, Galashiels, by 1880 and was still listed there in 1977. By 1984 McQueen Printers Limited were listed at Buckholm Print Works, Nether Road, Galashiels TD1 3HE and the company remained there until they ceased trading circa 2001. Additional premises were known in 1984 at 77, Albert Place, Galashiels, in 1993 at Units 4/5, Tweedmouth Industrial Estate, Galashiels and in 1997 at Langlee Industrial Estate, Galashiels. McQueen Printers Limited (company SC60338) was registered on 9th July 1976 and changed its name on 3rd March 1986 to McQueen Limited and on 20th March 1990 changed its name back to McQueen Printers Limited, before on 9th February 1995 changing its name again to McQueen Escot Trustees Limited. The company was dissolved on 22nd February 2002.

23. The imprint printed at the **Northern Chronicle Office, Inverness** is known on a ticket of the Highland Railway. They were first listed in directories in 1893 at 47, High Street, Inverness. By 1904 they were listed at Margaret Street, Inverness where they were still listed in 1950, but they ceased trading sometime after this date.

24.* The imprint **Pandaprint, Dunfermline** is known on the reverse of a ticket issued for a trip on the boat Maid of the Forth. Pandaprint were based at Netherton Broad Street, Dunfermline Fife but they moved premises circa 1999 and at the same time they changed the company name to Envoy Printed Communications 104. Park Road, Rosyth, Dunfermline Fife KY11 2JL

25.* The imprint **Hugh Paton & Sons Ltd, Edinburgh** is known on a ticket of Scottish Motor Traction issued in 1939.

Their factory was situated at 4/5, St. James Square, Edinburgh 1, from where they were trading as early as 1872, and as late as 1950. No trace could be found in directories by 1960, however the company (company SC9915) was not dissolved until 14/7/1989. An office was also known on Princes Street, Edinburgh from 1872 to 1889.

26. The imprint **Print Plus** is known on the reverse of the Ayr Buzz Card of Western Scottish and on the reverse of a pass of Stagecoach of Perth. This pass predates the take over of Western Scottish by Stagecoach Holdings. Print Plus was the in-house printing arm of Western Scottish that had previously been known Western Print the change of name taking place circa 1990. Print Plus informed me that printing work had also taken place for former Scottish Bus Group Companies, Midland, Kelvin, Central and Clydeside but I have yet to see any of their tickets bearing this imprint. They were based at Nursery Avenue, Kilmarnock KA1 3JD but they are no longer trading.

27.* The imprint **The Print Machine Tel: 33773** is known on weekly tickets of The Harte Bus Company of Greenock, Renfrewshire. A similar imprint but including the STD code 0475 is also known on weekly tickets of both Argyll Bus and Coach Ltd, and Pride of the Clyde Coaches Ltd. The Print Machine was based at 6, John Street, Gourock, Renfrewshire but is no longer trading having ceased in the past decade.

28.* The imprint **H & A Ritchie**, 10, Hanover Street Edinburgh is known on a ticket of the Edinburgh and Northern Railway (see page 4). Hugh and Alexander Ritchie traded at 10, Hanover Street, Edinburgh from 1847-1849. In 1850 Alexander Ritchie moved to 19, South St. David Street, Edinburgh where he stopped until 1875. In 1874 the name was changed to Alexander Ritchie and Son. From 1876 until at least 1973 the company were situated at 51, York Place, Edinburgh but by 1984 they had moved to their current premises at 161-163, Bonnington Road, Pilrig, Leith, Edinburgh EH6 5BQ. Alexander Ritchie & Son Limited (SC27956) was registered on 17/10/1950.

29. Tickets with the imprint **Ritchie P.P. Ltd, Klmk.** are known with Wallace's Motor Services of Largs. The company was earlier known as Ritchie Paper Products Ltd with premises situated at South West Stationery Works, John Finnie Street, Kilmarnock, by 1950. Ritchie Print Pack Ltd (SC13382) was registered on 14/11/1924 and changed its name on 1/6/1990 to Ritchie (UK) Ltd. and again on 1/2/1996 to Ritmark Ltd. They had moved to South Western Works, Hurlford Road, Riccarton, Kilmarnock KA1 4LA, by 1970, from where they are still trading. Despite changes to the company name this company is still listed under printers and lithographers in Yellow Pages as Ritchie UK Ltd.

(17) W.M. MacDonald

(20) Maclure and MacDonald

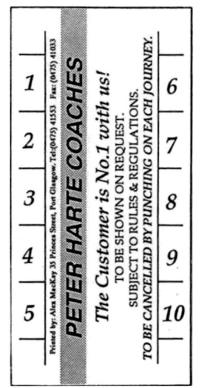

(18) Alex MacKay

(24) Pandaprint

Earnside Coaches – Glenfarg, Perth

PUPILS SEASON TICKET

SESSION ....

FROM .... TO ....

SERVICE NO. .... VALID UNTIL ....

PUPILS NAME ....

John McKinlay, Printer, Perth

(19) John McKinlay

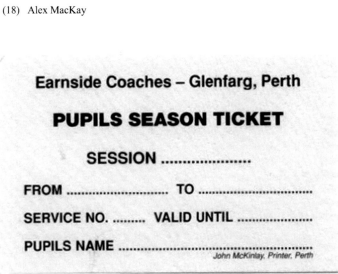

(25) Hugh Paton & Sons Ltd

30.* **P.Scrogie Ltd. (SC8814)** was registered on 4/10/1913. Their imprint is known on punch tickets of James Sutherland of Peterhead. Peter Scrogie was first seen listed in Kelly's 1893 directory at Broad Street, Peterhead, but by 1900 he had moved to his current premises which is situated at Buchan Observer Office, 17, Chapel Street, Peterhead, Aberdeenshire AB42 6TJ.

31.* The imprint **SCWS Ltd Printers** is known on a punch ticket of Skye Transport, Portree, Isle of Skye. The proprietors also being SCWS Ltd. Scottish Co-operative Society Ltd were based at 95, Morrison Street, Glasgow, although the printing department was situated at 71, Kingston Street, Glasgow. The printing works have now closed.

32. The imprint **Shetland News** is known on a ticket of J. Leask and Son of Lerwick. Shetland. Shetland News, the printers of the Shetland Times traded from premises at Prince Alfred Street, Lerwick, Shetland. The Shetland News Ltd. (SC136224) was dissolved on 24/8/1993.

33.* The imprint **Stevens, East Riggs** is known on a punch ticket of Richard Percival Limited of Carlisle. East Riggs is a small village near Annan in Dumfriesshire but so far I have been unable to find any trace of this printer in directories.

34.* The imprint **Strathclyde Printing Company, Saltcoats** is known on the reverse of a ticket of Clyde Coast Services Ltd, of Saltcoats, Ayrshire. Strathclyde Printing Services are no longer trading having operated from premises situated at 26, Hamilton Street, Saltcoats Ayrshire.

35. **Viking Printers**.........................see C.Billette.

(27) The Print Machine

(31) SCWS Ltd

(34) Strathclyde Printing Company

(30) P. Scrogie Ltd

WELSH IMPRINTS

1. The imprint **Allens** and initials **ASL** are known on Mid Glamorgan concessionary passes and City of Cardiff Transport tickets. Allens Printers and Stationers Ltd. (co 877370) was registered on 21/4/1966 with the registered office situated at Lermon Court, Fairway House, Links Business Park, St, Mellons, Cardiff CF3 0LT. Prior to 27/3/1997 the company was known as Allens (Stationers) Ltd. with premises on Sloper Road, Cardiff.

2.* The imprint **AST Print Group** is known on a receipt of Cardiff City Transport Services Limited. Whilst the illustrated ticket was used for lost property no doubt the tickets could also be used for transport purposes. AST Print Group Limited is a fairly recent company (co 3068020) which was registered on 12th June 1995 and their only premises so far are the current premises at Ipswich Road, Roath, Cardiff, CF23 9AQ.

3.* The imprint **Barmouth Printers** is known on tickets issued for the Mid Wales Festival of Transport in 1983. Barmouth Printers have premises situated at Park Road, Barmouth Gwynedd LL42 1PH from where they are still trading.

4.* The imprint **George Bell, Printer, Newport** is known on a transfer ticket of Lewis and James Ltd. George Bell claimed to have been established in 1872, but the first directory in which I have first found him listed was Kelly's in 1889 where he is at 61, Commercial Street, Newport, but by 1895 he had moved to 53, Commercial Street, Newport, where he remained until at least 1962. No trace could be found of this printer in directories by 1968.

5. **D. Brown and Sons Ltd.**(company 442593) was incorporated on 23/9/1947 trading at that time from premises at Eastgate Printing Works, 62, Eastgate, Cowbridge, Glamorgan CF7 7YA. They were still at these premises in 1970; however by 1975 they were at North Road Industrial Estate, Bridgend, South Glamorgan. The registered office is currently situated at 14, High Street, Cowbridge, South Glamorgan CF7 7AG. The company's initials are known on a duty pass of Western Welsh Omnibus Co Ltd and the full name is known on tickets of Red and White Services Ltd.

6.* The imprint **Caxton Press, Treorchy** is known on a weekly ticket of E.M.Williams of Treorchy. The Caxton Press were listed in directories for many years without an address just showing the town Treorchy but mentioning proprietor T.Evans. Recent directories however show Caxton Press, Howard Street, Treorchy, Mid Glamorgan CF42 6AR.

7.* The imprint **Criterion Press, Haverfordwest**, is known on a ticket of DG & PS Smith of Broadhaven. Criterion Press have ceased trading but had premises at Criterion Printing Works, Bridge Street, Haverfordwest, Dyfed, by 1961 from where they were still trading into the 1970's.

8. The imprint **Davies Cwmgorse** is known on tickets of W.T.Jones of Brynamman and Russell of Brynamman. D.Davies had premises at 73, Church Street Cwmgorse, Glamorgan. but have now ceased trading.

9.* The imprint **Ernest Davies and Co Ltd. Swansea** is known on a brake van permit of Burry Port and Gwendraeth Valley Railway. Ernest Davies and Co was first listed in 1893 at Goat Street, Swansea and was still here in 1936. There were also premises at 21/22, Fisher Street, Swansea (1899-1924). They had moved to 87, Brynymor Road, Swansea, by 1950 and were still there in the 1970's but have now ceased trading. In addition to the above limited company Ernest Davies & Co (1919) Limited has been seen in directories.

10.* The imprint **TTS Eastside** and **Eastside Printers** are known on tickets of Swansea Vale Railway. The company now trade only as Eastside Printers. The TTS prefix, stood for Tote Ticket Specialists. Eastside Printers Company Limited (company 4597211) was registered on 21/11/2002 with registered office situated at 219, Port Tennant Road, Port Tennant, Swansea SA1 8JU. This is the only known address for this printer.

11. The imprint **Wesca** is known on tickets of Inter Valley Link, Mid Glamorgan County Council and Rhymney Valley District Council issued in the 1970's and 1980's. This was the imprint of Walter Ellis and Son (Printers) Ltd. Being the initial letters plus CA from the town of Caerphilly. The company (685357) was registered on 6/3/1961 with the registered office at Windsor Hall, Windsor Street, Caerphilly. The company was dissolved on 22/6/1995. Prior to becoming a limited company there were premises at The Twyn, Caerphilly.

12.* The imprint **D Caradog Evans, Printer, Pwllheli**, is known on a ticket of Tocia Motor Omnibus Co Ltd. Daniel Caradog Evans is first listed in 1904 at 67, High Street, Pwllheli where he was still listed in 1948. In 1951 he was at Highlands, Salem Terrace, Pwllheli. He had vanished from directories by 1958. Dilwyn Chambers has evidence that Evans printed Pwllheli Corporation Tramways tickets, but I have not been seen these tickets.

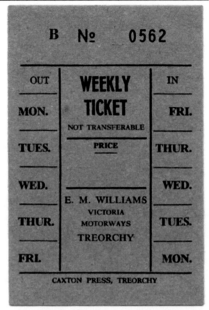

CARDIFF CITY TRANSPORT SERVICES LTD.

No 44656   Date 23-1-04

RECEIVED WITH THANKS

from Mr Wright

in respect of lost Property

amount in words Sixty Pence

£ — : 60 P

Signed by ....

on behalf of Cardiff City Transport Services Ltd.

VAT No. 655 6025 35

(2) AST Print Group

B № 0562

OUT	**WEEKLY**	IN
MON.	**TICKET**	FRI.
	NOT TRANSFERABLE	
TUES.	PRICE	THUR.
WED.		WED.
	E. M. WILLIAMS	
	VICTORIA	
THUR.	MOTORWAYS	TUES.
	TREORCHY	
FRI.		MON.

CAXTON PRESS, TREORCHY

(6) Caxton Press

MID WALES FESTIVAL OF TRANSPORT 1983

TICKET FOR

Festival Fleet Service No. _____

From .... Departing at ....

To ....

On .... Day .... June 1983

Fare .... **TICKET №** 0700

Issued subject to
published conditions.

(3) Barmouth Printers

№ R0173 Swansea Vale Railway **ADULT**

T.T.S. Eastside Printers

(10) T.T.S. Eastside Printers

Tocia Motor Omnibus Co., Ltd.

PWLLHELI.
and
ABERDARON 3/6 1042
Return Ticket.

The Company cannot be held responsible for any
irregularity in the service.

D. Caradog Evans, Printer, Pwllheli.

(12) D Caradog Evans

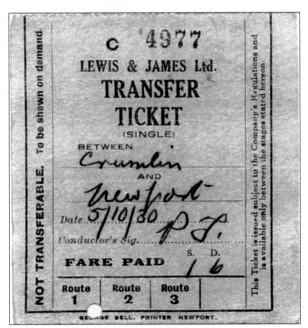

c 4977

LEWIS & JAMES Ltd.

TRANSFER TICKET

(SINGLE)

BETWEEN

Crumlin

AND

Newport

Date 5/10/30   P J.

Conductor's Sig. ....

FARE PAID   S. D. 1 6

Route 1	Route 2	Route 3

NOT TRANSFERABLE. To be shown on demand.

This Ticket is issued subject to the Company's Regulations and is available only between the stages stated hereon.

GEORGE BELL, PRINTER NEWPORT.

(4) George Bell Printer

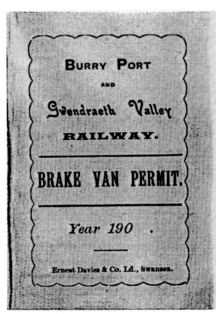

BURRY PORT

AND

Gwendraeth Valley

RAILWAY.

BRAKE VAN PERMIT.

Year 190 .

Ernest Davies & Co. Ld., Swansea.

(9) Ernest Davies & Co. Ltd.

13.* The imprint **E&ST** is known on tickets of West Monmouthshire Omnibus Board of Blackwood and Caerphilly UDC. This was the imprint of Evans and Short Ltd. Evans and Short Ltd (company 507775) was dissolved on 7/7/1987. They also printed posters for Rhondda Transport Co of Porth but no tickets from this company bearing this imprint are known. The company was registered in early 1952 and premises are known at Leader Works, Tonypandy (directories 1950-1975), Golden Grove, Newbridge, Monmouthshire. (directories 1961-1970), 1. West View, Newbridge (1950), and also at 123, Dewinton Street, Tonypandy.

14. The imprint **F.Hodge & Co Ltd. Cardiff** is known on a break of journey ticket issued by Red and White Services of Chepstow in the 1930's. F. Hodge and Company Ltd (Company 262529) was registered in early 1932 and was dissolved on 7/8/1971. Frank Hodge was first seen listed in 1907 at Plasnewydd Road, Cardiff. In 1909 Frank Hodge Limited was shown at the previous premises as well as Wyndham Arcade, Cardiff. In 1918 Hodge & Co were listed just at Wyndham Arcade, Cardiff. By the 1930's Hodge was at Gladstone Street, Cardiff, and later at 1.Tunnel Buildings, Queen Street, Cardiff (1936-1956), and Mardy Street, Grange, Cardiff by 1961.

15. The imprint **Island Press, Llanelli** is known on a season ticket of Rees and Williams of Tycroes, Ammanford. Island Press were based at Falcon House, Thomas Street, Llanelli Dyfed. This is yet another company to have ceased trading in recent years.

16. The imprint **E.G.Jenkins, printer, Blaina** is known on a weekly ticket of Williams Services. Jenkins has ceased trading and searches of old directories only give the name of the village but no street name for the printer

17. The imprint **D.W.Jones (Printers) Ltd., Port Talbot** is known on a season ticket of Thomas Bros. of Port Talbot. D.W.Jones (Printer) Ltd. (company 431740) was registered on 25/3/1947. Premises were then at 7A. Courtland Place, Port Talbot where they remained until the 1970's. The company is now at Empire Buildings, Beverley Street, Port Talbot SA13 1DY, where they have been since at least 1977.

18.* The imprint **Jones and Williams, Printer Wrexham** is known on a weekly ticket of Johnson's buses, Southsea, Wrexham. Jones and Williams (Printers) Ltd. (company 702878) was registered on 11/9/1961 with registered office situated at 69. Rhosddu Road, Wrexham LL11 2NW.

19. The imprint **Journal Works, Russell Road, Rhyl** is known on a ticket of The Royal Motor Coaches which show the printers address as Russell Road, Rhyl. This ticket was issued during the 1920's. Rhyl Journal was situated at 30. High Street, Rhyl by 1885 and they were still listed there in 1903, but by 1904 they had moved to 29. Russell Road, Rhyl where they were still situated in 1979.

Rhyl Journal is currently situated at 23. Kinmel Street, Rhyl. LL19 1AH where they have been since 1979.

20. The imprint **William Lewis, Duke Street, Cardiff** is known on a ticket of Taff Valley Railway. Lewis and Williams are listed in 1872 at Duke Street, Cardiff. William Lewis was first seen listed in his sole name in 1876 at 22. Duke Street, Cardiff, but by 1936 he had moved to 39/45. Penarth Road, Cardiff where he was still trading into the 1970's. Premises are also listed in directories at 70. Melrose Avenue, Cardiff (1950/1960); 67, Shirley Road, Cardiff (1950); 78. Queen Street, Cardiff (1936-1960) and 39. Kyle Crescent, Whitchurch (1961). Later directories show a limited company William Lewis (Printers) Limited. The company had ceased trading by 1977.

21. The imprint **WTM Co F** is known on the reverse of a Western Welsh season ticket. This was the imprint of W.T.Maddock & Co. The Printing Works, Ferndale, Glamorgan. The company is another to recently cease trading.

22.* The imprint **Mullock and Sons** is known on the reverse of Newport Corporation weekly tickets. Henry Mullock was trading from 16. Commercial Street, Newport by 1852. (Richard Mullock was here in 1849 but he was not a printer). He remained there until at least 1895, but by 1899 he had moved to Austin Friars, Newport where he remained into the 1960's, but by 1970 they had premises situated at 42. Argyle Street, Newport, Gwent. Mullock & Son also had premises in Mount Stuart Square, Cardiff in 1907-1909, and by 1918 had moved to 20. Working Street, Cardiff. Mullock & Son Limited (company 76723) was registered on 17/3/1903. On 15/8/2000 this company changed its name to Argyle Developments (Newport) Ltd. With the registered office situated at 47. Albany Street, Newport, Gwent, NP20 5NG. On 7/9/2000 another company (4067009) was registered Mullock & Sons Ltd. This is a dormant company with the registered office situated at 6. Ty Verlon Industrial Estate, Barry, Vale of Glamorgan, CF63 2BE.

23.* The imprint **Neath Printing Co. Charlesville Place, Neath** is known on a pass from the Neath and Brecon Railway issued in 1920. Harry W Rees was established in 1867 and he traded from Charlesville Place, Neath, From 1899 onwards The Neath Printing Company are listed at Charlesville Place, Neath, and they were still at these premises in 1992, however they had ceased trading by 1995.

24. **Park Business Forms Ltd.** (company 2048218) was registered on 20/8/1986 with registered office situated at 2. Glynstell Close, Hadfield Road, Cardiff, CF1 8AW. Their imprint was known on the reverse of Cardiff City Transport tickets during the 1980's. The company was dissolved recently on 9/4/2002.

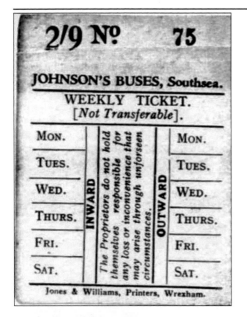

2/9 № 75

JOHNSON'S BUSES, Southsea.
WEEKLY TICKET.
[Not Transferable].

INWARD		OUTWARD	
MON.		MON.	
TUES.	The Proprietors do not hold themselves responsible for any loss or inconvenience that may arise through unforseen circumstances.	TUES.	
WED.		WED.	
THURS.		THURS.	
FRI.		FRI.	
SAT.		SAT.	

Jones & Williams, Printers, Wrexham.

(18)   Jones & Williams, Printers

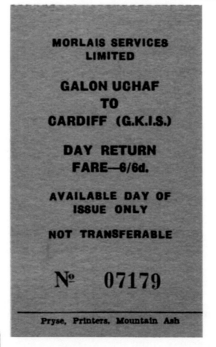

MORLAIS SERVICES LIMITED

GALON UCHAF TO CARDIFF (G.K.I.S.)

DAY RETURN FARE—6/6d.

AVAILABLE DAY OF ISSUE ONLY

NOT TRANSFERABLE

№ 07179

Pryse, Printers, Mountain Ash

(27)   Pryse Printers

NEWPORT CORPORATION TRANSPORT

This ticket must be produced on every journey. Failure to do so will require the passenger to pay the appropriate fare.

NOT TRANSFERABLE

MULLOCK & SONS, LTD.

(22)   Mullock & Sons, Ltd

No. ....

WEST MON. OMNIBUS BOARD

OLD AGE PENSIONERS' CONCESSIONAL FARE

PERMIT

E. C. PUGH, General Manager
Board Offices, Blackwood

E&S.T.

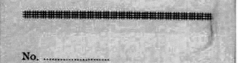

(13)   E & S.T.

Llwynypia Workingmen's Club Ltd.

Children's Annual Outing to Porthcawl

ON SATURDAY, JUNE 1st, 1963
Buses leave Club at 9.30 a.m.   Return 6 p.m.

Member's Ticket   № 587

Pentre Printing Co.

(26)   Pentre Printing Co.

NEATH AND BRECON RAILWAY.

No......1126.

FREE PASS.—THIRD CLASS.

(NOT TRANSFERABLE.)   Available for One Journey Only in each direction.

Pass Mr....J.Price...

from......Craigynos......................to..........Neath.............

Outwards on......Sept............19 20...Return on....Sept............19 20.

Subject to the Conditions printed on the face and back hereof.

Neath Printing Co., Charlesville Place, Neath.

O. TALBOT.

Secretary and General Manager.....

This pass is available for use on or before the date specified above, but not afterwards; if used on a subsequent date, it will be forfeited, and the holder required to pay the full fare. If not used it must be returned to the Officer of the Company by whom it was issued.

(23)   Neath Printing Co.

25. The imprint **PC Business Forms Ltd** is known on tickets of Berry's of Taunton. PC Business Forms Limited (company 1739941) was registered on 15th July 1983. The company has been situated at 3. Moor Street, Chepstow, Monmouthshire, NP16 5DF since they commenced trading in 1983 and they are still there today. The company informs me that they have printed coach tickets for several operators in addition to Berry's. The company now uses the trading name PCF Secure Document Systems.

26.* The imprint **Pentre Printing Co.** is known on a ticket issued by Llwynypia Working Men's Club during 1963. Pentre Printing Company is no longer trading, but they had premises situated at 10. Llewellyn Street, Pentre, Glamorgan.

27.* The imprints **Pryse & Son, Mountain Ash** and **Pryse Printers, Mountain Ash** are both known on tickets of Morlais Services Ltd. David Jenkin Pryse was first seen listed in 1939, at 22A. Oxford Street, Mountain Ash, but he then vanished from directories, *(serving in forces?),* until he reappeared in 1948 at Ffrwd Crescent, Mountain Ash, and he was still there in 1975. D.J.Pryse and Son had moved to Duffryn Road, Mountain Ash, Glamorgan by 1977 and he remained there until he ceased trading in the 1990's. By 1991 they also had premises at 39. Cannon Street, Aberdare, and 84. High Street, Merthyr Tydfil.

28.* The imprint **F.Pullen Printer Knighton 'phone 61** is known on a pass issued by Radnorshire Motor Services, Knighton. Reg Pullen is listed at 4. Station Road, Knighton, Radnorshire since 1916 and was still listed there in 1963 and had the same telephone number as F Pullen. He had ceased trading by 1967.

29. **Seargeant Bros Printers Ltd.** (company 1670813) was registered on 11/10/1982 with premises at Unit 12. Pontyfelin Road Industrial Estate, New Inn, Pontypool, Gwent NP4 0DQ. And earlier address being Unit 9, on the same industrial estate but I don't know whether they moved units or just renumbered them. Their initials are known on Mid Glamorgan concessionary passes of the 1980's

30.* The imprints **J. Seary & Co Newport,** and **Seary Ltd.** Are known on tickets of Newport Corporation Transport. The company was formed in 1917 by Frank Seary and his two sons Victor and John. The only known premises are at 10. Caerleon Road, Newport, Gwent NP19 7BU. Seary Printers (Newport) Limited (company 658066) was registered on 3/5/1960

31.* The imprint of **HWS & S** is known on a tickets of Gelligaer UDC and West Monmouthshire Omnibus Board. HWS&S was the imprint of Harry Wood Southey and Sons Ltd. who had premises at 110. High Street, Merthyr by 1872 and by 1904 at Express Buildings, Glebeland Street, Merthyr, where they were still situated in 1961. They had ceased trading by 1970. Roy Marshall the former general manager at Gelligaer confirmed my research into this printers initials.

32.* The imprint **S'PRINT** is known on a coach ticket of Davies Bros of Pencader Dyfed. S'PRINT had premises at 16. Ralph Street, Llanelli, Dyfed at the time ticket was printed but later moved to 15. Inkerman Street, Llanelli, Dyfed SA15 3RY. The company has recently ceased trading, vanishing from directories in 2003.

33.* The imprint **Sylric Press** is known on tickets of a miniature railway in Roath Park, Cardiff. Sylric Press had premises at 24. Letty Street, Cardiff by 1961 and were still there in the 1970's but by 1977 they moved to 13A. Fanny Street, Cardiff. This is yet another printer to cease trading in the last decade.

34. The imprint **Teifi Press Cardigan** is known on a coach ticket of Richards Bros. Moylegrove, Cardigan. Teifi Press have premises situated at 32. Feidr Fair, Cardigan, Dyfed, SA43 1ED, although they now trade under the name Gwasg Teifi Press.

35.* The imprints **TTS** and **TTS Monmouth,** are known on tickets produced by Transport Ticket Services, of Yew Tree Cottage, Newcastle, Monmouth, Gwent, NP5 4NU. Tony Green the proprietor of TTS (Transport Ticket Services) who is also a member of the TTS (Transport Ticket Society), commenced printing of tickets in 1982 with a weekly ticket for Evans of New Tredegar and a 10 journey ticket for Roy Grindle of Cinderford. Tickets have since then been produced for a number of operators although Tony informs me that printing is secondary to the supply and repair of ticket machines.

36.* The imprint **Valleyprint Anglesey** is known on a boarding card of B&I Line. Valley Print had premises at Valley Mill, Valley, Anglesey. This is yet another printer to disappear in the last decade.

37.* The imprint **Walkey Thomas & Co Ltd. Cardiff** is known on a ticket of Taff Valley Railway issued in 1917. Thomas Walkey and Co Ltd. was listed in 1895 at 43. Waterloo Street, Cardiff but by 1899 he was trading from premises at Tudor Street, Cardiff and was still listed there in 1936, but by 1939 he had vanished from directories.

CONDITIONS OF ISSUE.

1.—This Ticket must be kept clean, and signed below photograph by the holder.

2.—No preferential treatment will be accorded the holder of this Ticket.

3.—This Ticket will not guarantee a seat in any 'bus or even admittance to any 'bus which has its full complement of pass'gers.

4.—The Proprietors will not accept any liability or responsibility for delays or consequential damages arising from any cause whatever.

5.—This Ticket remains the property of Radnorshire Motor Services, who reserve the right to cancel it at any time. It must be handed in for renewal on expiry or in the event of the employee leaving the firm's services it must be surrendered immediately.

6. Children of employees must surrender this Pass immediately upon leaving school.

F. PULLEN, PRINTER, KNIGHTON. 'PHONE 51.

HALF FARE PASS

No._____

(*Not Transferable*)

Radnorshire Motor Services KNIGHTON.

To be shown on demand.

(28) F. Pullen

Nº ___ 9049   /B

EVANS COACHES LTD
Tel. Bargoed 834249

WEEKLY TICKET

Fare Paid £ __6__

Valid from___ 21 MAR 1986

Valid Until_____

Issued subject to Company's rules and regulations

TTS MONMOUTH

(35) TTS Monmouth

CONDITIONS

Available ONLY for one journey to school and return per day.

Not available for MID-DAY travel except on special occasions when journey FROM school is necessary because of school closure after morning session.

Not available after 5.30 p.m.

This ticket must be shown on every journey

This ticket expires on

_____

Seary Ltd   17/71

Voucher Ticket

issued in conjunction with

Newport Corporation Transport Department

F. Thorp,
General Manager

(30) J. Seary

GELLIGAER URBAN DISTRICT COUNCIL
Omnibus Service Season Ticket
(Not Transferable)

No. C 495   Rate £ 1 : 8 : 6

Mr C. J. Collins

From 3 : 10 : 64 : ___ to

-2 NOV 1964

Between BARGOED P.O. and FLEUR-DE-LIS

Via _____

This Ticket must be produced on request and is to be given up on expiry.
HWS&S 56947

(31) HWS&S

B&I LINE Boarding Card

TO BE PRESENTED UPON DEMAND

HOLYHEAD - DUBLIN

O   Nº 11660

Please see reverse

VALLEYPRINT, ANGLESEY TEL. (0407) 740070

(36) Valleyprint

38. **WAP Printers Ltd.** (company 423461) was registered on 11/111946 with premises at Old Regal Cinema, Regal House, Court Road, Barry, South Glamorgan. Their imprint is known on Mid Glamorgan concessionary passes. The company was dissolved on 17/12/1996. Another company (3002831) WAP Printers (Barry) Ltd was also dissolved on 3/11/1998. This company only existed with this name since 8/2/1995 having earlier been called Porta Coffee Ltd. Despite being registered as a limited company in 1946 I have been unable to find any trace of this company in telephone directories in the 1950-1970 periods which may signify a change of name or location.

39. The imprint **Watkins Ltd. Swansea** is known on a workman's privilege ticket of Llanelly and Mynydd Mawr Railway Co. I have found three printers in Swansea by the name of Watkins and as all have ceased trading I have been unable to ascertain which printed this ticket. H.Watkins, printer is listed in 1881at 4. Raynors Place, Swansea, and by 1899 they are listed as Watkins Limited at the same address but they had vanished from directories by 1904. Watkins Printing Company Limited was trading from 1. Castle Square, Swansea from 1920-1924 but had ceased by 1936. Watkins Printing and Stationery Company Limited (W.J.Watkins) were at 4-5. Rutland Street, Swansea from 1899-1924 but had disappeared from directories by 1936.

40.* The imprints **W.Whittington Ltd Neath** is known on a tickets of United Welsh Services Ltd. W.Whittington Ltd company 241383) was registered on 29/7/1929. On 31/12/1978 the company name changed to W. Whittington, Cyfyngedig. Walter Whittington was first seen listed in 1856 at Church Street, Neath and London Road, Neath, but by 1865 he had moved to 49. Wind Street, Neath, Glamorgan where he remained until the company ceased trading.

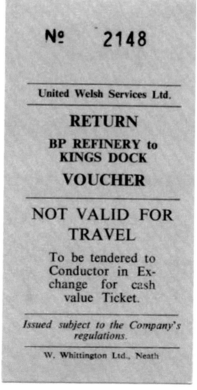

(33) Sylric Press

(37) Walkley Thomas & Co. Ltd

(40) W. Whittington

ISLAND IMPRINTS

(1) Isle of Man Imprints

* The imprint **Bridson & Horrox, Douglas,** is known on a weekly ticket of Manx Electric Railway. Bridson & Horrox was formed by Marshal Bridson and Harry Horrox in 1933. The company is still trading today as Bridson Horrox traded from 1. Market Street, Douglas from 1933 until circa 1992 when they moved to their current premises situated at Print House, Hills Meadow, Douglas, Isle of Man, IM1 5EB.

• The imprint **Brown & Sons Ltd.** And also their initials are known on the reverse of tickets of the Isle of Man Railways and Isle of Man Road Services. Brown and Sons Ltd had premises situated at Athol Street, Douglas (1900-1927) and 51. Victoria Street, Douglas (1912-1927). I could find no trace of this printer by1929.

• **IBC** is known on the tickets of Isle of Man National Transport Ltd. IBC printers was first seen listed in 1978 at 6. Fort William, Douglas, where they were still listed in 1980. They had moved to Lord Street, Douglas by 1985 where they remained until 1989 when they moved to M & G House, Head Road, Douglas where they were still listed in 1991, but they had ceased trading by 1996.

* The imprint **IDC Ltd.** Is known on parcel tickets of Isle of Man Road Services Ltd used during the 1970's. IDC was the imprint of Island Development Co Ltd. who had premises listed at Hill Street, Douglas in 1970. The company appears to have been short lived as it can't be found in either the 1967 or 1975 telephone directories.

• The imprint **Nelson Press Co. Ltd.** Is known on souvenir tickets of Douglas Corporation Transport and on tickets of Isle of Man Passenger Transport from the 1980's. Nelson Press Co. Ltd. Were first seen listed at 6. Senna Road, Douglas in 1955, and they were still listed there in 1958, but they had moved to 11. Market Street, Douglas by 1962 where they were still listed in 1964.

They had moved again by 1967 to 4. North Quay, Douglas where they were still listed in 1980, but by 1982 they had moved again to 13. St. George Street, Douglas where they were still listed in 1985. They had moved to their final premises by 1987 at Kingswood Grove, Douglas, IM1 3LY where they remained until they ceased trading during 2004.

• The imprint **NMP** is known on a runabout ticket issued by Isle of Man Railway. NMP was the imprint of Norris Modern Press. Originally the company was known as Norris Meyer Press however by 1916 it had changed its name to Norris Modern Press. *(anti-German feeling during the war?). Although a printer Louis Meyer is listed at 36. North Quay, Douglas for the first time in the 1916 directory, so he may have left the firm.* The company was listed at 7. Walpole Avenue, Douglas from 1912 until 1921, but it had moved to 6. Victoria Street, Douglas by 1924, and they were still listed there in 1989. The company had ceased trading by 1991. Additional premises are also listed in 1927 at 19. Castle Street, Douglas.

* The imprint and initials of **Quine & Cubbon** are known on parcel tickets of Isle of Man National Transport Ltd. Quine & Cubbon were first seen listed at Church Road, Port Erin in 1938 and they remained at these premises until 1979 when they moved to their current premises at 1. Athol Street, Port St. Mary, IM9 5DS. The firm was started as a partnership between Paddy Quine and a Mr Cubbon, (whose first name nobody at the company could remember when I contacted them). A limited company Quine and Cubbon Limited has subsequently been formed.

Sources-

Kelly's Directory for years 1900/1904/1912/1916/1919/1921/1924/1927.

Isle of Man Telephone Directories for the following years;

1929/38/44/48/50/52/53/55/58/62/64/67/70/75/78/80/82/85/87/88/89/91/92/96/99/2003/04

Isle of Man
Road Services Ltd.

PARCEL

Date 2 3 AUG 1972

20p

PAID

N⁰   2190

I.D.C. Ltd.

I.D.C. Ltd

ISLAND IMPRINTS

(2)   Channel Island Imprints

Guernsey

*   The imprint **Guernsey Press,** is known on punch tickets of Guernsey Motors Ltd and the imprint GP printers are known on a ticket of JMT. Guernsey Press and GP Printers have premises situated at Braye Road Vale, Guernsey, and also at 1. West Centre, St. Helier, Jersey. Earlier addresses known were 17. Pollet Street, St. Peters Port (1900) , 4-8. Smith Street, St. Peters Port (1904-1927) and le Marchant Street, St. Peters Port, Guernsey (1916-1927)

Jersey

•   The imprint **Commercial Art Co. Ltd.** Is known on tickets of JMT. Co. Ltd. Commercial Art Co. Ltd. Had premises situated at Bagatelle Road, St. Saviour, Jersey. The company are no longer trading.

Sources-

Kelly's Directory for years
1900/1904/1912/1916/1919/1921/1924/1927.

Telephone Directories; 1989/2003

*   The imprint **Wardleys** is known on tickets of Sarre Transport Ltd. William Henry Wardley had premises at 2. Trinty Square, St Peters Port (1900), 9. Mill Street, St. Peters Port (1904.), 15.Mansell Street, St. Peters Port (1912-1919), and 22. High Street, St. Peters Port (1921-1927). Later WH Wardley had premises at Rectory House, St. Peters Port, Guernsey until the mid 1950's when the company ceased trading.

IRISH PRINTERS IMPRINTS
Northern Ireland

•   The imprint **BL & C Ltd.** is known on the reverse of a ticket of Great Northern railway Board Omnibus Services from 1958. BL & C Ltd. was the imprint of Bell, Logan and Carswell Ltd (company NI R614) of 35-39. Queens Street, Belfast. The firm was founded in the mid 1950's as a result of a merger of Robert Carswell and Sons Ltd of 35-39. Queen Street, Belfast and Bell & Logan Ltd of Linen Hall Street, Belfast. The company remained at these premises until at least 1980, however no trace could be found of the company in directories by 1985.

*   The imprint **RC & S Ltd. B** is known on a ticket of Great Northern Railway (Ireland). This is the imprint of Robert Carswell and Sons Ltd (See Above), of 27 Donegal Place, Belfast (1876-1880), Royal Avenue, Belfast (1889-1893), and 35-39 Queen Street, Belfast (1900-1955). Premises are also listed at 70A Basinghall Street, London, (1914), and 31. Drury Street, Dublin (1919).

*   The imprint **Counties Advert Co, Belfast** Is known on tickets of Spences Triumph Auto Service and Sloane's Bus Service. Counties Advertising Co had premises situated at 30. Rosemary Street, Belfast by 1927 and were still listed there in 1930, but had vanished from directories by 1938. (See Seabrooke opposite)

*   The imprint **Seabrooke Printer, Belfast** is known on a ticket of Belfast and Newry Motor Service. W Seabrooke had premises at 30, Rosemary Street, Belfast and was listed there in the February 1926 telephone directory, but by August 1926 directory they were listed as Seabrooke and Rusk Limited. Kelly's 1927 directory lists Counties Advertising Company at this address, all three firms having Belfast 1019 as the telephone number.

•   The imprint **W & SM (I) Ltd** is known on an excess fare ticket of Great Northern Railway Board. This is the imprint of W & S Magowan (Ireland) Limited (company NI 402) William & Samuel Magowan were first seen listed in 1876 at 46. Hill Street, Newry where they were still listed in 1889. They were listed at 106. Hill Street, Newry by 1893 and were still at these premises in 1962. Later premises were at Edward Street, Newry listed from 1947 to 1985. Other addresses known are at 19.Bedford Street, Belfast which was listed from 1947 to 1980 and 21. Ormeau Avenue, Belfast (1985). The company was dissolved on 15th April 1994.

Isle of Man *(continued)*

MANX ELECTRIC RAILWAY

Available for 6 Return Journeys within 7 days from date of issue

OUT		IN
6		6
5		5
4		4
3		3
2		2
1		1

WEEKLY TICKET No. L 454

Issued to..

Available between..

and..

Issued..194......

E. BARNES General Manager & Engineer.

Per..

This ticket is granted subject to user conforming to the conditions as set out on the other side. Any person departing therefrom will have his ticket cancelled at once and when afterwards travelling on a car will be charged Ordinary Fare.

Bridson & Horrox, Douglas

Bridson & Horrox

Isle of Man
National Transport Ltd.

PARCEL

Date..

plus V.A.T

60p

PAID

No. 6902

Quine & Cubbon

Quine & Cubbon

Guernsey

Express
ONE DAY TRAVEL CARD

1. Issued subject to the regulations and conditions published in the Company's Official Time Table.
2. Available for unlimited travel on all services detailed in the Company's Official Time Table.
3. Tickets must be shown to the conductor or any of the Company's Officials on demand.
4. No refunds are allowed.
5. Tickets are personal and are **not transferable**, and remain the property of the Company.
6. This ticket does not entitle the holder to claim priority to travel.
7. Valid for one day as shown.

GP PRINTERS GUERNSEY C.I.

GP Printers

Jersey

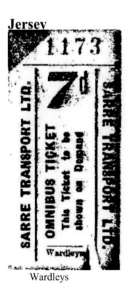

Wardleys

Northern Ireland

This series of Tickets is Not Transferable and is issued subject to the Regulations of each Company over whose Railways, Steamboats, or Coaches any of the Tickets may be available, and to the Conditions in their Time Tables and Tourist announcements. These Tickets, unless where otherwise stated, do not include the cost of transfer between Railway Termini or Steamboats. The Tickets must not be separated by the person to whom they are issued, but by the Ticket Collector.

R. C. & S., LTD., B.

Passengers are allowed One Week to complete their Journey.
Each Ticket is available for One Journey only. This COVER to be given up with last Ticket. No allowance made for Tickets lost or not used.

ENNISKILLEN (G.N.R.I.) TO GLASGOW (Cal. Ser.) A

SINGLE FARE, 12s. 9d.

THIRD CLASS AND STEERAGE.

Date issued :

No. 510

R.C. & S. Ltd. B

In conclusion…..

The vast majority of printer I contacted were very helpful; some were more helpful than others as is the case in life generally. In fact a few went well out of their way to help me but there is always one exception and there was only the one out of all the printers I contacted. I had a photocopy of a ticket giving the imprint **EBF Cards** and a telephone number. I rang the telephone number and all started well, they confirmed that they printed the ticket, in fact they stated that they had printed tickets for several bus companies. I was intrigued and asked "who else they had printed tickets for?" I was informed that this information was commercially confidential and they couldn't tell me. OK, fair enough I could have been a rival printer. So my next question was "What does EBF stand for?" I was then informed that they could not tell me as this information was commercially confidential. This was a new one on me and sensing I was getting nowhere I terminated the call. Five minutes later I rang the company again, the same man's voice was on the end of the phone and he answered "Essex Business Forms" to which I said "is that Essex Business Forms" He replied "yes" so I put the receiver down having got the information I required. In fairness to this company other people I have spoken to have reasonably helpful but this individual clearly does not believe that enthusiasts exist who would be interested in tickets. I've spoken to him three times now in the past decade and I've got the same response each time!

Another peril of research is demonstrated by the hours that I have spent looking through Irish printer's directories for a printer with the initials "ON". I found these on a CIE ticket. I had to admit defeat and then I decided to contact Cyril McIntyre whom I thought would know the answer to this question if anyone did. And yes, he did; the initials ON stood for order number!

There are a couple of imprints that have been reported to me that so far, that I have not a photocopy of,

- Simpson   Beach Model Railway, Carnoustie
- Beacon Printer, Penarth   SA Bebb Ltd

If anyone present today can help, I would be very grateful……….

Finally my favourite imprint illustrated on the front cover of this publication. A car park ticket and the imprint "HENRY PRINTED IT".

I would like to give special thanks to Paul Smith for proof reading this address and to David Harman for preparing the slides used for the illustrations.

I have decided to do two things different with this presidential address. Firstly I am going to hand out a copy of this address to those present instead of waiting for it to be printed. Secondly, I have also included a further section that I have prepared on Islands and Ireland. This just leaves by far the largest section of all, England, to be completed some time in the future, although much research has already been done. It should be cautioned that directories of the Channel Islands are not readily available in England for research, so only a limited number have been consulted.

Counties Advert   Seabrooke Printer